Anthony Murphy

CRUISE SHIP JOBS

Get a Job on a Cruise Ship-within a month, even if you have zero experience.

Thanks for buying my book!

Aloha!

My name is Anthony Murphy.

I have had the pleasure of working aboard 9 cruise ships (as well as 6 tug boats and one Bering Sea fishing vessel).

When I first decided to work on ships I found there wasn't much info out there on how to get and keep a job.. and most of what there was wasn't very realistic.

The goal of this book is to give you a "quick and dirty" guide to getting a job..AND a realistic idea of what it is like once you are aboard.

This book is INTENTIONALLY short. I wanted to give you everything you need to know- in less than an hour.

If you have additional question or suggestions-please email me @ amurphy719@gmail.com

Standing lookout in the Great Lakes as our mate gives a bridge tour to passengers

First things first

Before you start applying using the info contained in later pages- you need to answer the following questions honestly;

1 Are you able to prove that you are a US citizen?
The info in this book applies only to US flagged cruise ships which, by law, can ONLY hire US workers.
*Please note-

Most of the big cruise ships you've seen- including Disney, Carnival, Royal Caribbean, etc. are registered in other countries, are NOT subject to US LABOR LAWS....
AND...

DO NOT PAY NEARLY AS MUCH as US flagged ships!

They also have longer contracts (also called rotations) of up to 1 year and even longer work hours than US ships.

The last ship I worked aboard in an paid me $150 day ($4,500 per month) as a deckhand. I was offered a similar position with a foreign flagged ship-at $600 per month.

Some foreign ships also save money by "hot bunking" which means you sleep in a bunk..then another crewmember sleeps there when you are working. Not very appealing to me!

(If you still want to work on a foreign flagged ship-shoot me an email and I will send you info)

2-Are you 18 plus?
Again- required..and some companies require 21 plus.

3- Are you physically capable of working 12 plus hour days ,7 days per week(no days off), for weeks or months at a time?

4- Are you willing and able to work hard, with a positive attitude, while working and living in close quarters with people who may or may not be like you?

*You WILL work with people of all backgrounds, religions, political affiliations,ethnicities, musical tastes, sexual orientations,etc...and discrimination is NOT allowed.

5- If you drink or smoke-are you willing to refrain from it while working? Drinking,smoking, chewing, and electronic cigarette use while on duty are not allowed. Depending on the company- you may or may not be allowed to drink while off work/off the ship. NCL has a crew bar for use after work-but you are never allowed to drink in guest bars,in public areas,or in your room. Even on ships that allow drinking- you are NEVER allowed to exceed .04 blood alcohol content(Federal Law for crew) or to be disruptive,loud, or act "drunk"

Some ships have designated smoking areas..some don't. Smoking anywhere else WILL get you fired

Working on ships is..well..a LOT of work! You will work 12 or more hours per day, EVERY day, for weeks or months straight- and share a room with one or more other workers.

You are expected to act professionally on and off duty. I like to think of cruise ships as a cross between the military and a resort- there is a chain of command that you must follow,there are uniforms, superior officers (who can give you orders you must legally follow) and emergency drills that you MUST take part in.

Unlike regular jobs your job doesn't end when your shift does- there may be drills, training, loading or unloading stores (supplies) ,trash, etc. In an emergency you will be expected to assist in emergency response as well. You will go many beautiful places and you will have time off- but it is a job.

Drills-

Me- after a fire drill on a ship in the Pacific Northwest

Every crewmember on any ship has two jobs- the one you were hired for (waiter, deckhand,bartender, Captain,etc) and,more importantly, CREWMEMBER. On a ship the crew is the fire department,medical first responder,and security force.

You are expected (and required by law) to be able to respond in the event of an emergency. Each crewmember is assigned duties for each type of emergency.You will be trained how to respond in emergencies including fire, man overboard, and abandon ship.You may also be trained/drilled in security,medical response, pollution response, and damage control.

There are usually two drills- one just before/just after the cruise begins (for the passengers and crew) and one in the middle of the week/cruise for crew only which mayor may not be announce be announced. You may be off shift- or even asleep when the alarm goes off- you still have to show up.I have awoken many times in the middle of the night to the general alarm blaring- some were drills- some were real. Take it seriously. If you don't you are putting your job,your safety, and the safety of everyone on the ship in danger.

Stores,Luggage and Trash

Most or all of the crew (depending on the ship) are responsible for bringing aboard supplies, called "stores" or "provisions" as well as assisting passengers and their luggage on and off the ship at the beginning and end of the cruise.On smaller ships you may also be asked to help with trash. Trash must be stored on the ship (in approved areas)

This is hard, sweaty work. Look at it as free weekly exercise!:-)There's no better way to make your shipmates dislike you than to disappear when it's time for stores!

Crew Areas vs Passenger Areas

There are two main areas on cruise ships- passenger areas (most of the ship) and crew areas.

In general- passengers can not go in crew areas..and crew (unless working can't go in passenger areas except in the performance of job duties. Crew usually has their own dining area (usually called a crew mess) separate laundry area, etc. Some small ships have shared dining areas- passengers eat, then crew.

Space on ships is at a premium. Almost everything is smaller- especially in the crew area. Unless you are a captain, officer, or manager- you will probably share a room with 1-5 others.

Rooms usually have bunkbeds with privacy curtains,lockers, and a small shared bathroom/shower. Most (not all) have a tv with basic cable. A few of the larger ships (Notably NCL's Pride of America) have a crew lounge, crew bar,crew gym,etc...but most do not.

You MUST keep your room clean and be respectful of roommates- who may be sleeping while you are off shift.

The cruise line CAN AND WILL inspect your room-usually weekly! If you do not pass inspection you may not be allowed off the ship until the room is clean and reinspected.

Meals and laundry are free. Most ships have free laundry soap. Meals are usually pretty good ..but not the same as what passengers get. Some ships also have 24hr free soda, juice,fruit,cereal, coffee,tea,sandwiches, soup,etc..but this varies from ship to ship,

Deckhand meeting on the M/V Yorktown- I am second from left. :-)

  The people who don't last in the cruise industry are the ones who forget this truth- "You may be on a cruise ship- but you are NOT on a cruise!" If you are looking for an easy job ..or a vacation- YOU WILL BE DISAPPOINTED.

APPLYING

Am I qualified?

The biggest lie that most books and websites tell is -

"It's hard to get a job on a cruise ship"

The exact opposite is true.

There is a lot of turnover.The job ISN'T for everyone..and LOTS of people quit when they realize it is work..not vacation.:-)

Assuming you meet the basic criteria mentioned earlier, are flexible as far as which ship and position you will accept, and keep applying/following up- you will get hired. It may take the cruise line hours..or months to get back to you- make sure you are packed- and ready to go at any time.

I once got a call when I was sitting in a coffee shop on the island of Kauai asking if I could be at the airport in 30 minutes. I ran, caught a ride, and flew to Oregon where I boarded a ship bound for Alaska.

Be prepared! :-)

*Apply online first,then look on their website for a job fair, then follow up online!

How to ACE the Interview

All companies will ask slightly different questions.. but are looking for the same basic answers ;

1-Can you do the job?Answer by mentioning relevant experience.

And most importantly-

2-Will you be able to handle long hours,tight living quarters, being part of a diverse team, being away from home participating in a chain of command,etc..

How you answer this question WILL determine if you get hired.

Keep repeating how you did ANYTHING similar in the past!!

Military,boy scouts/girl scouts,farming, construction, over

the road trucking,working in another state...ANYTHING similar helps! :-)

Positions onboard

The following list is from Blount and shows basic positions common to ships.It is NOT all inclusive. The larger the ship- the more crew and positions. NCL's Pride of America, for example, has almost 1,000 total crew (counting entertainers) and many different levels of employee in each department. Even the dishwashers have managers and officers!

Captain:
Responsible for overseeing all crew and operations on the vessel to which they are assigned. The Master shall operate the vessel with the safety of the passengers, the crew and the environment foremost in mind. Captains for Blount Small Ship Adventures require both managerial and hands on skills. As a Captain on a Blount Small Ship Adventures vessel, you will assist in the training of crew, the piloting of the vessel itself as well as the smaller vessels of the ship and in inspecting the vessel and its components. Captains are also responsible for interacting with our passengers at certain functions as well as providing narration via the ship's PA system in certain areas that we travel through.

First Mate:

Supervises, trains and coordinates activities of the deck department. Responsible for assisting in the piloting, navigation, safety, first aid, cleanliness and small boat operations. Responsibilities include training employees, planning, assigning and directing work, appraising performance, rewarding and disciplining employees, addressing complaints and resolving problems.

Engineer:

Responsible for the maintenance, operations and repair of all the vessel's electrical and mechanical systems onboard ships. Keeps vessels maintenance records and inventories. Makes proposals for maintenance and repair projects.

Cruise Director/Purser:

Responsible for overseeing all staff and functions within the hotel department. Coordinates all passenger activities both on board the vessel and off the vessel in each port and handles public relations for the ship. Manages the shipboard accounting, administrative and clerical duties. Responsible for handling Customs and Immigration for the vessel.

Chef:

Responsible for all staff and functions within the galley and the coordination of meal service including three guest meals and three crew meals per day. The Chef will coordinate all galley activities in regards to food preparation, inventory, menu planning, preparing the food, cleaning, training, food ordering and storage.

Assistant Chef:

Responsible for preparing and serving meals with the Chef. Primary responsibilities are baking, salad and appetizer preparation and desserts. Maintain proper galley sanitation and safety standards. Bake breads daily, as well as muffins, pastries, etc., for the snack trays and any additional baking that is required by the Chef. Responsible for maintaining cleanliness and order in all food storage areas including galley stores and other storage areas. Assist with loading of food stores. Baking experience preferred.

Stewardess/Steward:

Responsibilities include dining room set-up, service and clean up of all meals. Works in the Galley on a rotating basis washing dishes and general galley clean up. Cleans the guest cabins on a daily basis, including making beds, vacuuming and cleaning the bathrooms. Interacting with the passengers on a daily basis must have good customer service skills.

Deckhand:

Responsibilities include maintenance of the vessels exterior and interior, which may include painting, sweeping, window washing and vacuuming; Luggage handling, participating in docking and anchoring maneuvers and line handling; Standing Watches (wheel, gangway, deck, fog, anchor)for security purposes; engine room system checks.

"But I have never worked on a ship!"

Doesn't matter for entry level positions- though mention experience if you have it. Most of the employees haven't worked on the water either. :-)

Where do you want to go?

Most US flagged cruiselines ONLY go to US ports. There are a few that go to Canada, Baja Mexico, and the Caribbean/Central America. Additionally- a few of the companies also have internationally flagged sister ships- so you may possibly be able to travel abroad- if you ask-though at much lower pay as mentioned earlier.

The following is a current list of US flagged cruise providers providing overnight cruises as well as info on where they sail. It does not include foreign flagged companies or cruises that only go out for the day.

Norwegian Cruise Line America(NCLA)

NCLA operates 7 day cruises in the Hawaiian Islands(Oahu,Big Island,Maui,and Kauai)aboard the largest US flagged cruise ship "Pride of America"

I recommend applying at NCL first for several reasons-

1-They have job fairs nationwide.Much easier to get hired in person. 2- They pay for training(BST) and special ID (MMC and

TWIC) that you will need with certain companies/positions.

3-They are one of the easiest places to get a "foot in the door" of the industry

*TIP- If you have little or no hotel,restaurant,or bar experience- apply for a "utility" position- IE utility galley (dishwasher) Utility bar (barback) Utility hotel (janitor in guest areas) or utility stores (warehousing on ship) You can move up fast if you are a good, hard worker.:-)

http://www.ncl.com/about/careers/shipboard-employment-pride-of-america/how-to-apply

Hr email-
shipboardemployment@ncl.com

The American Empress

American Queen Steamboat Company

AQSC operates two paddlewheel riverboats- one in the Pacific Northwest..and one on the Mississippi River and its many tributaries. They are the second and third largest US flagged cruise ships. Due to weather where they sail they do not offer year round employment.

How to apply-

http://www.americanqueensteamboatcompany.com/Contact-Us/Career-Opportunities/

hr@hmsgm.com or call 1-812-941-9990 Ext.125

Blount Cruises

Blount travels as far north as Canada and the US Great Lakes , as far South as the Caribbean,and many small ports along the East Coast. Because of their itineraries you may be able to work year round- if you have a passport.

http://www.blountsmallshipadventures.com/contact-us/employment/

American Cruise Lines

American Cruise Lines (ACL) offers small ship cruises in Alaska, the Pacific Northwest,and along the US East Coast from Maine to Florida, including New York City. They hire online , but your best bet is at one of their job fairs.

Pluses- easy to get hired as a deckhand or steward (combination waiter housekeeper) with ZERO experience. They have a foreign flagged sister company- Pearl Seas cruises-if you want to sail internationally.

Negatives- They hire for 12 weeks- after that-you go home.I have seen exceptions- but usually not a place that hires long term. Not the same level of training as at other companies.

http://www.americancruiselines.com/employment

Tip-Look on their website and apply in person at a job fair.I applied online several times- never heard back.Was hired immediately at the job fair. They don't sail in the winter-but you may be able to work in the shipyard before and after the season.

They often hold job fairs in-

Guilford, CT (Headquarters)		
Salt Lake City,UT		
Houston, TX		
Phoenix, AZ		
Sandy, UT		
Austin, TX		
Orlando, FL		
Portland, OR		

Un-Cruise Adventures

Un-Cruise offers Cruises in Alaska, the Pacific Northwest, and seasonal cruises to Hawaii and Baja Mexico.

They pride themselves on being different than the other cruise lines and offer more of

a nature themed cruise featuring kayaking,hiking,etc.

__Careers@Un-Cruise.com

Alaskan Dream Cruises

Alaskan Dream Cruises ONLY does Alaska.They pride themselves on this.

Apply at-

http://www.alaskandreamcruises.com/contact-us/employment-opportunities/

Lindblad/NationalGeographic

Lindblad Expeditions has Partnered with National Geographic to offer wilderness and ecology cruises throughout the world.They have many ships- but only the Sea Lion and Sea Bird are US flagged.

They sail to Alaska,The Pacific Northwest,Baja Mexico,Panama Canal, and Costa Rica- depending on the time of the year… You need a passport for this company.

More info and application links here-
http://www.expeditions.com/about-us/employment/

or email them -lexjobs@expeditions.com

That's it from me..the rest is up to YOU! :-)

Fair winds and following seas!

Anthony
amurphy719@gmail.com

| |
| |
| |
| |
| |